THE MORTAL DANGER

The Oak and the Calf
A World Split Apart
The Gulag Archipelago I–II
The Gulag Archipelago III–IV
The Gulag Archipelago V–VII
Prussian Nights
Warning to the West
Lenin in Zurich
Letter to the Soviet Leaders
Candle in the Wind
The Nobel Lecture on Literature
August 1914
A Lenten Letter to Pimen, Patriarch of All Russia
Stories and Prose Poems
The Love Girl and the Innocent
Cancer Ward
The First Circle
For the Good of the Cause
We Never Make Mistakes
One Day in the Life of Ivan Denisovich

Aleksandr I. Solzhenitsyn

THE MORTAL DANGER

HOW MISCONCEPTIONS ABOUT RUSSIA IMPERIL AMERICA

TRANSLATED FROM THE RUSSIAN BY
Michael Nicholson and Alexis Klimoff

1817

HARPER & ROW, PUBLISHERS, New York
Cambridge, Hagerstown, Philadelphia, San Francisco,
London, Mexico City, São Paulo, Sydney

This work was originally published in *Foreign Affairs*, Vol. 58, No. 4 (Spring 1980), under the title "Misconceptions About Russia Are a Threat to America." The translation has been slightly revised for the present edition.

FIRST EDITION

Designer: Sidney Feinberg

LIBRARY OF CONGRESS CATALOG CARD NUMBER: 80–7919
ISBN: 0–06–014043–7
    0–06–090828–7 pbk

---

80 81 82 83 84 10 9 8 7 6 5 4 3 2 1

THE MORTAL DANGER

1.

Two Fallacies About Communism

Anyone not hopelessly blinded by his own illusions must recognize that the West today finds itself in a crisis, perhaps even in mortal danger. One could point to numerous particular causes or trace the specific stages over the last sixty years that have led to the present state of affairs. But the ultimate cause clearly lies in sixty years of obstinate blindness to the true nature of communism.

I am not concerned here with those who cherish, glorify, and defend communism to this day. To such people I have nothing to say. Yet there are many others who are aware that communism is an evil and a menace to the world, but who have nevertheless failed to grasp its implacable nature. And such individuals, in their capacities as policy advisers and political leaders, are even now committing fresh blunders which will inevitably have lethal repercussions in the future.

Two mistakes are especially common. One is the failure to understand the radical hostility of communism to mankind as a whole—the failure to realize that communism is irredeemable, that there exist no "better" variants of communism; that it is incapable of growing "kinder," that it cannot survive as an ideology without using terror, and that, consequently, to coexist with communism on the same planet is impossible. Either it will spread, cancer-like, to destroy mankind, or else mankind will have to rid itself of communism (and even then face lengthy treatment for secondary tumors).

The second and equally prevalent mistake is to assume an indissoluble link between the universal disease of communism and the country where it first seized control—Russia. This error skews one's perception of the threat and cripples all attempts to respond sensibly to it, thus leaving the West disarmed. This misinterpretation is fraught with tragic consequences; it is imperiling every nation, Americans no less than Russians. One will not have to await the coming of future generations to hear curses flung at those who have implanted this misapprehension in the public awareness.

I have written and spoken at length about the first of these errors, and in so doing have aroused considerable skepticism in the West, but agreement seems to be increasing with the passage of time and as the lessons of history are assimilated.

The present essay is mainly devoted to the second fallacy.

2.

Russia and the U.S.S.R.

To begin with, there is the careless and inaccurate use of the words "Russia" and "Russian" in place of "U.S.S.R." and "Soviet." (There is even a persistent emotional bias against the former: "Russian tanks have entered Prague," "Russian imperialism," "Never trust the Russians," as against "Soviet achievements in space" and "the triumphs of the Soviet ballet.") Yet it ought to be clear that these concepts are not only opposites, but are *inimical*. "Russia" is to the Soviet Union as a man is to the disease afflicting him. We do not, after all, confuse a man with his illness; we do not refer to him by the name of that illness or curse him for it. After 1917, the state as a functioning whole—the country with its government, policies, and armed forces—can no longer be referred to as Russia. It is inappropriate to apply the word "Russian" to the present authorities in the U.S.S.R., to its army, or to its future military successes and regimes of occupation throughout the world, even though the official language in each case might be Russian. (This is equally true of both China and Vietnam, only in their case no equivalent of the

3

word "Soviet" is available.) A certain American diplomat recently exclaimed: "Let Brezhnev's Russian heart be run by an American pacemaker!" Quite wrong! He should have said "Soviet heart." Nationality is determined not by one's origins alone, but also by the direction of one's loyalties and affections. A Brezhnev who has connived at the ruin of his own people in the interests of foreign adventures has no Russian heart. All that his ilk have done—to destroy the national way of life and to pollute nature, to desecrate national shrines and monuments, and to keep the people in hunger and poverty for the last sixty years—shows that the communist leaders are alien to the people and indifferent to its suffering. (This is equally true of the ferocious Khmer Rouge, the Polish functionary who may have been reared by a Catholic mother, the young communist activist, taskmaster over a group of starving coolies, or the stolid Georges Marchais with his Kremlin-like exterior; each has turned his back on his own nationality and has embraced inhumanity.)

For present-day purposes the word "Russia" can serve only to designate an oppressed people which is denied the possibility of acting as one entity, or to denote its suppressed national consciousness, religion, and culture. Or else it can point to a future nation liberated from communism.

There was no such confusion in the 1920s when progressive Western opinion exulted over Bolshevism: the object of its enthusiasm was then named "Soviet" outright. During the tragic years of the Second World War, the concepts "Russian" and "Soviet" seem to have merged in the eyes of the world (a cruel error, which is discussed below). And with the coming of the cold war, the animosities generated were then directed principally toward the word "Russian." The effects are being felt to this day; in fact, new and bitter accusations have in recent years been leveled against all things "Russian."

3.

Ignorance Through Scholarship

The American reader receives his information about and forms his understanding of Russian history and the present-day Soviet Union chiefly from the following sources: American scholars (historians and Slavists), American diplomats, American correspondents in Moscow, and recent émigrés from the U.S.S.R. (I am not including Soviet propaganda publications, to which less credence is given lately, or the impressions of tourists, which, thanks to the skillful efforts of Intourist, remain altogether superficial.)

When American historical scholarship is confronted with the paucity of Soviet sources and with their Marxist distortion, then, for all its apparently unlimited scope and freedom from prejudice, it often unwittingly adopts the Procrustean framework provided by official Soviet historiography and, under the illusion of conducting independent research, involuntarily duplicates the approach and sometimes even the methodology of Soviet scholarship, in imitation of which it then duly skirts certain hidden and carefully hushed-up topics. It is sufficient to recall that until the most recent times the very existence of the Gulag Archipelago, its inhuman cruelty, its scope, its duration, and the sheer volume of death it generated, were not acknowledged by Western scholarship. To take a further example, the mighty outbreaks of spontaneous popular resistance to communism in our country between 1918 and 1922 have been quite disregarded by scholars in the West, and where they have been noted, they are termed "banditry," in line with Soviet parlance (for example, by Moshe Lewin).[1] In overall evaluations of Soviet history we still encounter the raptures with which "progressive" public opinion in Europe greeted the "dawning of a new life," even as the terrorism and destruction of 1917–1921 were at their height in our country. And to this day many American academics seriously refer to "the ideals of the revolution," when in fact these "ideals" manifested themselves from the very first in the murder of millions of people. Nor has Russia's distant past been spared the distorting effects of fervent radical thought in the West. In recent years American scholarship has been noticeably dominated by a most facile, one-dimensional approach, which consists in explaining the unique events of the twentieth century, first in Russia and then in other lands, not as something peculiar to communism, not as a phenomenon new to human history, but as if they derived from primordial Russian national characteristics established in some distant century. This is nothing less than a racist view. The events of the twentieth century are explained by flimsy and

[1] The reference is to Lewin's review of a book by Oliver H. Radkey, *The Unknown Civil War in Soviet Russia: A Study of the Green Movement in the Tambov Region, 1920-1921,* in *Slavic Review,* Vol. 36, No. 4 (Dec. 1977), pp. 682-683. [Tr. note]

8

superficial analogies drawn from the past. While communism was still the object of Western infatuation, it was hailed as the indisputable dawning of a new era. But ever since communism has had to be condemned, it has been ingeniously ascribed to the age-old Russian slave mentality.

This interpretation currently enjoys wide support, since it is so advantageous to many people: if the crimes and vices of communism are not inherent to it, but can be attributed entirely to the traditions of old Russia, then it follows that there exists no fundamental threat to the Western world; the rosy vistas of détente are preserved, together with trade and even friendship with communist countries, thereby ensuring continued comfort and security for the West; Western communists are freed from incrimination and suspicion ("they'll do a better job; theirs will be a really good communism"); and a burden falls from the conscience of those liberals and radicals who lent so much of their fervor and their assistance to this bloody regime in the past.

Scholars of this persuasion treat the history of the old Russia in a correspondingly peremptory manner. They permit themselves the most arbitrary selection of phenomena, facts, and persons, and accept unreliable or simply false versions of events. Even more striking is their almost total disregard for the spiritual history of a country that has been in existence for a thousand years, as though (as Marxists argue) this has had no bearing upon the course of its material history. It is regarded as essential when studying the history and culture of China or Thailand, or any African country, to feel some respect for the distinctive features of that culture. But when it comes to the thousand years of Eastern Christianity

9

in Russia, Western researchers by and large feel only astonishment and contempt: why ever did this strange world, an entire continent, persistently reject the Western view of things? Why did it refuse to follow the manifestly superior path of Western society? Russia is categorically condemned for every feature which distinguishes her from the West.

Richard Pipes's book *Russia Under the Old Regime*[2] may stand as typical of a long series of pronouncements that distort the image of Russia. Pipes shows a complete disregard for the spiritual life of the Russian people and its view of the world—Christianity. He examines entire centuries of Russian history without reference to Russian Orthodoxy and its leading proponents (suffice it to say that St. Sergius of Radonezh, whose influence upon centuries of Russian spiritual and public life was incomparably great, is not once mentioned in the book, while Nil Sorsky is presented in an anecdotal role).[3] Thus, instead of being shown the living being of a nation, we witness the dissection of a corpse. Pipes does devote one chapter to the Church itself, which he sees only as a civil institution and treats in the spirit of Soviet atheistic propaganda. This people and this country are presented as spiritually underdeveloped and motivated, from peasant to tsar, exclusively by crude material interests. Even within the sections devoted to individual topics there is no convincing,

---

[2] New York: Charles Scribner's Sons, 1974, 361 pp.

[3] Sergius of Radonezh (1314–1392), perhaps the best-loved Russian saint, combined mystical spirituality with a practical concern for the Russian nation. In 1380 he gave his blessing to Dmitri, Prince of Moscow, to fight in a battle that proved to be the first decisive Russian victory over the Mongol occupiers.

St. Nil Sorsky (Nilus of Sora, 1433–1508) represents the mystical and contemplative tradition of Eastern monasticism. He argued that the Church and the State should be independent of each other. [Tr. note]

logical portrayal of history, but only a chaotic jumble of epochs and events from various centuries, often without so much as a date. The author willfully ignores those events, persons, or aspects of Russian life which would not prove conducive to his thesis, which is that the entire history of Russia has had but a single purpose—the creation of a police state. He selects only that which contributes to his derisive and openly hostile description of Russian history and the Russian people. The book allows only one possible conclusion to be drawn: that the Russian nation is anti-human in its essence, that it has been good for nothing throughout its thousand years of history, and that as far as any future is concerned, it is obviously a hopeless case. Pipes even bestows upon Emperor Nicholas I the distinction of having invented totalitarianism. Leaving aside the fact that it was not until Lenin that totalitarianism was ever actually implemented, Mr. Pipes, with all his erudition, should have been able to indicate that the idea of the totalitarian state was first proposed by Hobbes in his *Leviathan* (the head of the state is here said to have dominion not only over the citizens' lives and property, but also over their *conscience*). Rousseau, too, had leanings in this direction when he declared the democratic state to be "unlimited sovereign" not only over the possessions of its citizens, but over their *person* as well.

As a writer who has spent his whole life immersed in the Russian language and Russian folklore, I am particularly pained by one of Pipes's "scholarly" techniques. From among some forty thousand Russian proverbs, which in their unity and their inner contradictions make up a dazzling literary and philosophical edifice, Pipes wrests those half doz-

11

en (in Maxim Gorky's tendentious selection) that suit his needs, and uses them to "prove" the cruel and cynical nature of the Russian peasantry. This method affects me in much the same way as I imagine Rostropovich would feel if he had to listen to a wolf playing the cello.

There are two names that are repeated from book to book and article to article with a mindless persistence by all the scholars and essayists of this tendency: Ivan the Terrible and Peter the Great, to whom—implicitly or explicitly—they reduce the whole sense of Russian history. But one could just as easily find two or three kings no whit less cruel in the histories of England, France, or Spain, or indeed of any country, and yet no one thinks of reducing the complexity of historical meaning to such figures alone. And in any case, no two monarchs can determine the history of a thousand-year-old nation. But the refrain continues. Some scholars use this technique to show that communism is possible only in countries with a "morally defective" history, others in order to remove the stigma from communism itself, laying the blame for its incorrect implementation upon Russian national characteristics. Such a view was voiced in a number of recent articles devoted to the centenary of Stalin's birth, for instance in a piece by Professor Robert C. Tucker (*The New York Times*, 21 December 1979).

Tucker's short but vigorous article is astounding: surely this must have been written twenty-five years ago! How can a scholar and student of politics persist to this day in misunderstanding so fundamentally the phenomenon of communism? We are confronted yet again with those familiar, never-fading ideals of the revolution, which the despicable

Stalin ruined by ignoring Marx in favor of the abominable
lessons of Russian history. Professor Tucker hastens to sal-
vage socialism by suggesting that Stalin was not, after all, a
genuine socialist! He did not act in accordance with Marxist
theories, but trod in the footsteps of that wearisome pair,
Ivan the Terrible from the sixteenth century and Peter the
Great from the eighteenth. The whole Stalin era, we are to
believe, is a *radical reversion* to the former tsarist era, and
in no wise represents a consistent application of Marxism to
contemporary realities; indeed, far from carrying on the
Bolshevik cause, Stalin contributed to its destruction. Modes-
ty prevents me from asking Professor Tucker to read at least
the first volume of *The Gulag Archipelago*, and better still
all three. But perhaps that would refresh his memory of how
the communist police apparatus which would eventually
grind up some sixty million victims was set up by Lenin,
Trotsky, and Dzerzhinsky, first in the form of the Cheka,
which had unlimited authority to execute unlimited num-
bers of people without trial; how Lenin drew up in his own
hand the future Article 58 of the Criminal Code, on which
the whole of Stalin's Gulag was founded;[4] and how the entire Red Terror and the repression of millions of peasants
were formulated by Lenin and Trotsky. *These* instructions,
at least, Stalin carried out conscientiously, albeit only to the
extent of his limited intellectual abilities. The only respect in
which he ventured to depart from Lenin was his destruction
of the Communist Party leadership for the purpose of
strengthening his own power. But even here he was merely

[4] On Lenin's contribution to the drafting of the Criminal Code, see *The
Gulag Archipelago*, Vol. I, pp. 352–354. [Tr. note]

enacting a universal law of vast and bloody revolutions, which invariably devour their own creators. In the Soviet Union it used to be said with good reason that "Stalin is Lenin today," and indeed the entire Stalin period is a direct continuation of the Lenin era, only more mature in terms of its results and its long, uninterrupted development. No "Stalinism" has ever existed, either in theory or in practice; there was never any such phenomenon or any such era. This concept was invented after 1956 by intellectuals of the European Left as a way of salvaging the "ideals" of communism. And only by some evil figment of the imagination could Stalin be called a "Russian nationalist"—this of the man who exterminated fifteen million of the best Russian peasants, who broke the back of the Russian peasantry, and thereby of Russia herself, and who sacrificed the lives of more than thirty million people in the Second World War, which he waged without regard for less profligate means of warfare, without grudging the lives of the people.

Just what "model" could Stalin have seen in the former, tsarist Russia, as Tucker has it? Camps there were none; the very concept was unknown. Long-stay prisons were very few in number, and hence political prisoners—with the exception of terrorist extremists, but including all the Bolsheviks—were sent off to exile, where they were well fed and cared for at the expense of the state, where no one forced them to work, and whence any who so wished could flee abroad without difficulty. But even if we consider the number of nonpolitical prisoners at forced labor in those days, we find that it amounted to less than one ten-thousandth of the population of Gulag. All criminal investigations were

14

conducted in strict compliance with established law, all trials were open and defendants were legally represented. The total number of secret police operatives in the whole country was less than that presently available to the KGB of the Ryazan district alone; secret police departments were located only in the three major cities and even there surveillance was weak, and anyone leaving the city limits immediately escaped observation. In the army there was no secret intelligence or surveillance whatsoever (a fact which greatly facilitated the February Revolution), since Nicholas II considered any activity of this type an insult to his army. To this we may add the absence of special border troops and fortified frontiers, and the complete freedom to emigrate.

In their presentation of prerevolutionary Russia, many Western historians succumb to a persistent but fallacious tradition, thereby to some extent echoing the arguments of Soviet propaganda. Before the outbreak of war in 1914, Russia could boast of a flourishing manufacturing industry, rapid growth, and a flexible, decentralized economy; its inhabitants were not constrained in their choice of economic activities, distinct progress was being made in the field of workers' legislation, and the material well-being of the peasants was at a level that has never been reached under the Soviet regime. Newspapers were free from preliminary political censorship (even during the war), there was complete cultural freedom, the intelligentsia was not restricted in its activity, religious and philosophical views of every shade were tolerated, and institutions of higher education enjoyed inviolable autonomy. Russia, with her many nationalities, knew no deportations of entire peoples and no armed separatist movements. This picture is not merely dissimilar to that of the communist era, but is in every respect its direct antithesis. Alexander I had even entered Paris with his army, but he did not annex an inch of European soil. Soviet conquerors never withdraw from any lands on which they once have set foot—and yet these are viewed as cognate phenomena! The "bad" Russia of old never loomed ominously over Europe, still less over America and Africa. She exported grain and butter, not arms and instructors in terrorism. And she collapsed out of loyalty to her Western allies, when Nicholas II prolonged the senseless war with Wilhelm instead of saving his country by concluding a separate peace (like Sadat today). Western animosity toward the former Russia was aroused by Russian revolutionaries in emigration, who propounded crude and simplistic views inspired by their political passions; these were never counterbalanced by responses or explanations from Russia, since no one there had any conception of the role of "agitation and propaganda." When, for example, on 9 January 1905, tragic events culminated in the death of about a hundred people during a St. Petersburg demonstration (no one was arrested), this came to be regarded as an inerasable stigma, a shameful episode which amply characterizes Russia. Yet the Soviet Union is not constantly reproached for the 17th of June 1953, when six hundred demonstrators in Berlin were killed in cold blood and fifty thousand more arrested. Indeed, such episodes seem to inspire respect for Soviet strength: "We must seek a common language."

Somehow, over the years, the friendship that existed between Russia and the young, newly formed United States in

16

the eighteenth century has been forgotten. Hostility toward Russia gained ground from the early twentieth century on. We are still witnessing its consequences today. But today these are much more than just remote sentiments; they threaten to lead the entire Western world into a fatal error.

4.

Misinformation by Informants

With American scholars demonstrating such a fundamental misunderstanding of Russia and the U.S.S.R., the blunders perpetrated by politicians come as less of a surprise. Although they are ostensibly men of action, their heads are ever under the sway of current theories and their hands shackled by the exigencies of the moment.

Only the combined effect of these factors can account for the notorious resolution on the "captive nations" (Public Law 86–90), passed by the U.S. Congress on 17 July 1959 and subsequently renewed: the manifest culprit, the U.S.S.R., is nowhere identified by name; world communism is referred to as "Russian"; Russia is charged with the subjugation of mainland China and Tibet and the Russians are denied a place on the roll of oppressed nations (which includes the nonexistent "Idel-Ural" and "Cossackia").

Ignorance and misunderstanding have clearly spread far beyond this one resolution.

Many present and former United States diplomats have also used their office and authority to help enshroud Soviet communism in a dangerous, explosive cloud of vaporous arguments and illusions. Much of this legacy stems from such diplomats of the Roosevelt school as Averell Harriman, who to this day assures gullible Americans that the Kremlin rulers are peace-loving men who just happen to be moved by heartfelt compassion for the wartime suffering of their Soviet people. (One need only recall the plight of the Crimean Tatars, who are still barred from returning to the Crimea for the sole reason that this would encroach upon Brezhnev's hunting estates.) In reality the Kremlin leadership is immeasurably indifferent to and remote from the Russian people, a people whom they have exploited to the point of total exhaustion and near extinction, and whom, when the need arises, they will mercilessly drive to destruction in their millions.

By means of his essays, public statements, and words of advice, all of which are supposedly rooted in a profound understanding of Soviet life, George Kennan has for years had a major detrimental influence upon the shape and direction of American foreign policy. He is one of the more persistent architects of the myth of the "moderates" in the Politburo, despite the fact that no such moderates have ever revealed themselves by so much as a hint. He is forever urging us to pay greater heed to the Soviet leaders' pronouncements and even today finds it inconceivable that anyone should mistrust Brezhnev's vigorous denials of aggressive intent. He prefers to ascribe the seizure of Afghanistan to the "defensive impulses" of the Soviet leadership. Many Western diplomats have abandoned painstaking analysis in favor of incurable self-delusion, as we can see in such a veteran of the political arena as Willy Brandt, whose *Ostpolitik* is suicidal for Germany. Yet these ruinous ventures are the very ones honored with Nobel Prizes for Peace.[5]

I would note here a tendency which might be called the "Kissinger syndrome," although it is by no means peculiar to him alone. Such individuals, while holding high office, pursue a policy of appeasement and capitulation, which sooner or later will cost the West many years and many lives, but immediately upon retirement the scales fall from their eyes and they begin to advocate firmness and resolution. How can this be? What caused the change? Enlightenment just doesn't come that suddenly! Might we not assume that they were well aware of the real state of affairs all along, but simply drifted with the political tide, clinging to their posts?

Long years of appeasement have invariably entailed the surrender of the West's positions and the bolstering of its adversary. Today we can assess on a global scale the achievement of the West's leading diplomats after thirty-five years of concerted effort: they have succeeded in strengthening the U.S.S.R. and Communist China in so many ways that only the ideological rift between those two regimes (for which the West can take no credit) still preserves the Western world from disaster. In other words, the survival of the West already depends on factors which are effectively beyond its control.

These diplomats still fall back on their precarious assumptions about an imaginary split within the Soviet Politburo

[5] The Nobel Peace Prize of 1971 was bestowed upon Willy Brandt, then the Chancellor of West Germany, for "concrete initiatives leading to the relaxation of tension" between East and West. [Tr. note]

between nonexistent "conservatives" and "liberals," "hawks" and "doves," "Right" and "Left," between old and young, bad and good—an exercise of surpassing futility. Never has the Politburo numbered a humane or peace-loving man among its members. The communist bureaucracy is not constituted to allow men of that caliber to rise to the top—they would instantly suffocate there.

Despite all this, America continues to be fed a soothing diet of fond hopes and illusions. Hopes have been expressed of a split in the Politburo, with one particular version claiming that it was not in fact Brezhnev who occupied Afghanistan! Or else leading experts have offered the fancy that "the U.S.S.R. will meet its Vietnam," be it in Angola, Ethiopia, or Afghanistan. (These experts and their readers may rest assured that the U.S.S.R. is at present quite capable of gobbling up five more such countries, swiftly and without choking.) And again and again we are asked to set our hopes on détente despite the trampling of yet another country. (There is indeed no cause for alarm here, for even after Afghanistan the Soviet leaders will be only too happy to restore détente to the *status quo ante*—an opportunity for them to purchase all that they require in between acts of aggression.)

It goes without saying that America will never understand the U.S.S.R. or fully grasp the danger it poses by relying on information from diplomats such as these.

But politicians of that ilk have lately been reinforced by recent émigrés from the Soviet Union, who have set about actively promoting their own spurious "explanation" of Russia and the U.S.S.R. There are no outstanding names among them, yet they earn prompt recognition as professors and

Russian specialists thanks to their sure sense of the kind of evidence that will find favor. They are persistent, outspoken, and repetitious contributors to the press of many countries, and the more or less concerted line which they take in their articles, interviews, and even books may be briefly summed up as follows: "collaboration with the communist government of the U.S.S.R., and war on Russian national consciousness." While these individuals were still in the U.S.S.R., they generally served the communist cause in various institutes, or were even actively employed for a number of years in the mendacious communist press, without ever voicing opposition. Then they emigrated from the Soviet Union on Israeli visas, without actually going to Israel (the Israelis term them "dropouts"). Having reached their destinations in the West, they immediately proclaimed themselves experts on Russia, on her history and national spirit, and on the life of the Russian people today—something they could not so much as observe from their privileged positions in Moscow. The most energetic of these new informants do not even blame the Soviet system for the sixty million lives it destroyed, or reproach it for its militant atheism. They condone its wholesale repression, while proclaiming Brezhnev a "peacemaker" and openly urging that the communist regime in the U.S.S.R. be given maximum support as the "lesser evil," the best alternative open to the West. Yet they simultaneously accuse the Russian national movement of this same kind of collaboration. The significance of the current spiritual processes in Russia is seriously misrepresented to the West. Western public opinion is being encouraged to respond with fear and even hatred to any revival in Russian national awareness, a sentiment that has been crushed almost to extinction by sixty years of communist power. In particular, contrived and disingenuous attempts have been made to link that revival with the government's calculated encouragement of anti-Semitism. For this purpose Soviet people are portrayed as nothing but a herd of sheep, utterly incapable of forming their own conclusions about their fate over the last sixty years or of understanding the cause of their poverty and suffering, entirely dependent upon official explanations from the communist leaders, and hence quite content to accept the anti-Semitic excuses which the government foists upon them. (In actual fact, the average Soviet citizen has a far shrewder understanding of the inhuman nature of communism than has many a Western essayist and politician.)

Several of these émigrés also indulge in rather uninformed digressions into earlier periods of Russian history, in close conformity with the above-mentioned myopic school of American historiography. Of the many members of this group we could here mention Dimitri Simes, or Alexander Yanov.[6] For seventeen years on end Yanov was a loyal communist journalist, who never spoke out against the regime, but now he glibly regales his credulous American readers

---

[6] Dimitri K. Simes was, until 1972, a staff member of the Institute of World Economy and International Relations in Moscow. He emigrated soon thereafter and is presently Director of Soviet Studies at Georgetown University's Center for Strategic and International Studies in Washington, D.C. He has written extensively on détente.

Alexander L. Yanov emigrated in 1974 and has been associated with the Institute of International Studies, University of California at Berkeley. He is the author of *Détente After Brezhnev* (1977) and *The Russian New Right* (1978). [Tr. note]

24

with distorted pictures of Soviet life or else skips lightly over
the surface of Russian history, studiously avoiding its fundamental principles and blowing out one soap bubble after another. Simultaneously, and on almost consecutive pages,
Yanov imputes to Russian national awareness two mutually
exclusive tendencies: messianism (a bizarre fabrication), and
isolationism, which for no apparent reason he regards as a
threat to the rest of the world.

Given that a hostile and distorted portrayal of old Russia
has been a tradition in American historical scholarship, seeds
such as these are capable of bearing poisonous fruit.

The efforts of these tendentious informants have been
supplemented and reinforced over the last year by a number
of articles written by American journalists and in particular
by the Moscow correspondents of American newspapers.
The gist of these articles is more of the same: the grave
threat which any rebirth of Russian national consciousness is
said to pose to the West; an unabashed blurring of distinc-
tions between Russian Orthodoxy and anti-Semitism (when
it is not explicitly claimed that the two are identical, they
are obtrusively juxtaposed in consecutive phrases and para-
graphs); finally there is the extraordinary theory according
to which the rising forces of national and religious consciousness and the declining, cynical communist leaders
have but a single dream—to merge together into some sort
of "New Right." The only puzzling question is what has
been stopping them from doing just that for all these years?
Who is there to forbid it? The truth of the matter is that religious and national circles in the U.S.S.R. have been systematically persecuted with the full force of the criminal code.

25

At first glance one is struck by how closely accounts by émigré informants and by free American correspondents coincide: if two independent sources report one and the same thing, then there must surely be something to it. But one must take into account the circumstances under which all Western correspondents have to operate in the Soviet Union: authentic Soviet life, especially life in the provinces and in the rural districts, is hidden from their view by an impenetrable wall; any trips they make out of the city are purely cosmetic, and are carefully stage-managed by the KGB; moreover, it is extremely hazardous for ordinary Soviet people in the provinces to engage in conversation with a foreigner, other than at the KGB's behest. Typical is Robert Kaiser's admission that in the four years he spent as Moscow correspondent of the *Washington Post* he had heard no mention whatever of the massive Novocherkassk uprising of 1962![7] The Western correspondent relies for his information upon the following: a careful screening of the vacuous and sterile official Soviet press; off-the-record comments and speculations gleaned from Western diplomats (the sources coincide!); and chance encounters with middle-level representatives of the Soviet elite (but as human material this is too shoddy and unreliable to merit serious attention). Their chief source, however, is the conversations they have with those few Muscovites who have already irrevocably violated the ban on fraternizing with foreigners; usually these are representatives of the same Moscow circles to which the aforementioned émigré informants once belonged. They are

---

[7] On the Novocherkassk uprising, see *The Gulag Archipelago*, Vol. III, pp. 507–514. [Tr. note]

the chief source of information used in strident, doom-laden articles about the worldwide menace of Russian nationalism. And this is how some anonymous anti-Semitic leaflet in a Moscow gateway is taken up by the Western press and invested with universal significance. But it also explains why the sources so often agree: an image of the world is formed in accordance with its reflection in a single splinter of glass. In physics this is known as systematic instrument error.

But when some information happens to point in a different direction, when it fails to tally with what the Western press is presently looking for in Moscow, then it is simply suppressed. A case in point is the extremely important interview that Igor Shafarevich gave to Christopher Wren of *The New York Times*, but that was not published in the Western press. In the same way Western scholars and the Western press have been ignoring the *Herald of the Russian Christian Movement* [*Vestnik Russkogo Khristianskogo Dvizheniia*], a Paris-based journal which has been appearing for half a century; yet the journal enjoys great popularity in cultivated circles and is in fact published with their direct participation. Acquaintance with this journal would give Western commentators quite a different picture, far removed from the horrors they are wont to describe.

Only this absence of informed opinion can account for the warped view that the main problem in the U.S.S.R. today is that of emigration. How can the problems of any major country be reduced to the issue of who is allowed to depart from it? Here and there in the Russian provinces (Perm was a recent example) strikes involving many thousands of starving workers have been dispersed by force of arms (para-

troops have even had to be dropped onto the factory roof)—
but is the West alert enough to note all this and to react to
it? And what of the far-reaching process that is now under
way in Russia and is scheduled for completion in ten to fifteen years, a process threatening the very survival of the
Russian people? It aims at nothing less than the final destruction of the Russian peasantry: huts and villages are being razed, peasants are being herded together in multi-
storied settlements on the industrial model, links with the
soil are being severed; national traditions, the national way
of life, even apparently the Russian landscape and the national character—all are disappearing forever. And the reaction of the meager Western news media to this murderous
communist onslaught on the very soul of our people? *They
have not so much as noticed it!* In the first revolution
(1917–1920), Lenin's curved dagger slashed at the throat of
Russia. Yet Russia survived. In the second revolution (1929–
1931) Stalin's sledgehammer strove to pound Russia to
dust. Yet Russia survived. The third and final revolution is
irrevocably under way, with Brezhnev's bulldozer bent on
scraping Russia from the face of the earth. And at this moment, when Russian nationhood is being destroyed without
pity, the Western media raise a hue and cry about the foremost threat to the world today—Russian national consciousness. . . .

5.

Russia Prostrate

Moscow is not the Soviet Union. Ever since the early 1930s, general living standards in the capital have been artificially boosted above the national level—by plundering the rest of the populace, particularly in rural areas. (The same is partially true of Leningrad and of certain restricted scientific settlements.) Thus for more than half a century the population of Moscow has had its diet artificially augmented and has been artificially maintained at a psychological level quite unlike that of the pillaged country at large. (The Bolsheviks learned the lesson of 1917, when the February Revolution broke out in hungry Petrograd.) As a result, Moscow has come to be a special little world, poised somewhere between the U.S.S.R. and the West: in terms of material comfort it is almost as superior to the rest of the Soviet Union as the West is superior to Moscow. However, this also means that any judgments based on Moscow experiences must be significantly corrected before they may be applied to Soviet experience in general. Authentic Soviet life is to be seen only in provincial towns, in rural areas, in the labor camps and in the harsh conditions of the peacetime army.

For my part, I spent the entire fifty-five years of my Soviet life in the remoter areas of the U.S.S.R., never enjoying the privileges of residence in the capital. I can thus draw upon my experiences without having to make any such correction, and my comments will consequently pertain not to Moscow, but to the country as a whole.

To begin with, the West's vision has been obscured by the false cliché according to which the Russians are the "ruling nationality" of the U.S.S.R. They are no such thing and never have been at any time since 1917. For the first fifteen years of Soviet power it fell to the Russians, Ukrainians, and Byelorussians to bear the crippling, devastating blow of communism (the declining birth rates of recent years have their roots in that period), and in the process their upper classes, clergy, cultural tradition, and intelligentsia, as well as the main food-producing section of the peasantry, were wiped out almost without trace. The finest names of the Russian past were outlawed and reviled, the country's history was systematically vilified, churches were obliterated in their tens of thousands, towns and streets were renamed in honor of executioners—a practice to be expected only of armies of occupation. But as the communists felt more firmly in control they dealt similar blows to each of the remaining national republics in turn, acting on a principle equally dear to Lenin, Hitler, and the common thug: always crush your enemies one by one. Thus in the U.S.S.R. there simply was no "ruling nationality": the communist internationalists never had need of one. The decision to retain Russian as the of-

30

ficial language was purely mechanical; one language after all had to serve in this capacity. The sole effect of this use of Russian has been to defile the language; it has not encouraged Russians to think of themselves as masters: just because a rapist addresses his victim in her own language, this does not make it any less of a rape. And the fact that from the end of the 1930s the communist leadership came to be increasingly composed of men of Russian and Ukrainian origin did absolutely nothing to raise those nations to hegemony. The same law operates throughout the world (in China too, and in Korea): to cast in one's lot with the communist leadership is to repudiate not only one's own nation but humankind itself.

But the bigger sheep yields more fleece, and so throughout the Soviet period it has been the R.S.F.S.R.[8] which has borne the main brunt of economic oppression. Fearing an outbreak of national resistance, the authorities were a little more cautious in applying economic measures to the other national republics. The inhuman kolkhoz system was installed everywhere; nevertheless, the profit margin on a hundredweight of oranges in Georgia was incomparably more favorable than that on a hundredweight of Russian potatoes harvested with greater expenditure of labor. Each of the republics was exploited without mercy, but the ultimate degree of exploitation was reached in the R.S.F.S.R., and today the most poverty-stricken rural areas of the U.S.S.R. are the Russian villages. The same is true of Russian provincial towns, which have not seen meat, butter, or eggs for decades

[8] R.S.F.S.R. is the official designation of that portion of the country which remains when the fourteen outlying "national republics" are excluded.

31

and which can only dream of even such simple fare as macaroni and margarine.

Subsistence at such an abysmally low level—for half a century!—is leading to a biological degeneration of the people, to a decline in its physical and spiritual powers, a process that is intensified by mind-numbing political propaganda, by the violent eradication of religion, by the suppression of every sign of culture, by a situation where drunkenness is the only form of freedom, where women are doubly exhausted (by working for the state on an equal footing with men and also in the home, without the aid of domestic appliances), and where the minds of its children are systematically deprived. Public morality has declined drastically, not due to any inherent failing in the people, but because the communists have denied it sustenance, both physical and spiritual, and have disposed of all those who could provide spiritual relief, above all the priesthood.

Russian national consciousness today has been suppressed and humiliated to an extraordinary degree by all that it has endured and continues to endure. It is the consciousness of a man whose long illness has brought him to the point of death and who can dream only of rest and recuperation. The thoughts and aspirations of a family in the depths of Russia are immeasurably more modest and timid than the Western correspondent can possibly gather from his leisurely Moscow chats. This is how their thoughts run: if only the petty local communist despot would somehow quit his uncontrolled tyranny; if only they could get enough to eat for once, and buy shoes for the children, and lay in enough fuel for the winter;

if only they could have sufficient space to live even two to a room; if only a church would be opened within a hundred miles of where they live; if only they weren't forbidden to baptize their children and bring them up knowing right from wrong; and if only they could get Father away from the bottle.

And it is *this* yearning on the part of the Russian hinterland to rise and live like men, not beasts, to regain some portion of its religious and national consciousness, which the West's glib and garrulous informants today label "Russian chauvinism" and the supreme threat to contemporary mankind, a menace greater by far than the well-fed dragon of communism whose paw is already raised, bristling with tanks and rockets, over what remains of our planet. It is *these* unfortunates, this mortally ill people, helpless to save itself from ruin, who are credited with fanatical messianism and militant nationalism!

This is just a phantom to scare the gullible. The simple love of one's mother country, an inborn feeling of patriotism, is today branded "Russian nationalism." But no one can possibly incite to militant nationalism a country that for fifty years has not even had enough bread to eat. It is not the average Russian who feels compelled to hold other nations captive, to keep Eastern Europe encaged, to seize and arm far-off lands; this answers only the malignant needs of the Politburo. As for "historical Russian messianism," this is contrived nonsense: it has been several centuries since any section of the government or intelligentsia influential in the spiritual life of the country has suffered from the disease of

Solved exactly

33

messianism. Indeed, it seems inconceivable to me that in our sordid age any people on earth would have the gall to deem itself "chosen."

All the peoples of the Soviet Union need a long period of convalescence after the ravages of communism, and for the Russian people, which endured the most violent and protracted onslaught of all, it will take perhaps 150 or 200 years of peace and national integrity to effect a recovery. But a Russia of peace and national integrity is inimical to the communist madness. A Russian national reawakening and liberation would mark the downfall of Soviet and with it of world communism. And Soviet communism is well aware that it is being abrogated by the Russian national consciousness. For those who genuinely love Russia no reconciliation with communism has ever been possible or ever will be. That is why communism has always been most ruthless of all in its treatment of Christians and advocates of national rebirth. In the early years this meant wholesale execution; later the victims were left to rot in the camps. But to this very day the persecution continues inexorably: Vladimir Shelkov was done to death by twenty-five years in the camps,[9] Ogurtsov has already served thirteen years and Osipov twelve;[10] this winter the completely apolitical "Christian Committee for the Defense of Believers' Rights in the

[9] Vladimir Shelkov, head of the independent branch of the Adventist Church in the Soviet Union, died in a strict-regime camp in January 1980. He was eighty-four years old. [Tr. note]

[10] Igor Ogurtsov headed an organization that advocated the rebuilding of Russia on Christian principles. Arrested in 1967, he was sentenced to twenty years of imprisonment and exile.

Vladimir Osipov, editor of *Veche*, a Samizdat journal dedicated to religious and nationalist themes, was sentenced to eight years in 1975. He had also served an earlier term for dissident activities. [Tr. note]

U.S.S.R." was smashed;[11] the independent priests Father Gleb Yakunin and Father Dimitri Dudko have been arrested,[12] and the members of Ogorodnikov's Christian seminar have been hauled off to prison.[13] The authorities make no attempt to hide the fact that they are crushing the Christian faith with the full force of their machinery of terror. And at this moment, when religious circles in the U.S.S.R. are being persecuted with such unmitigated ferocity—how fine and edifying it is to hear Russian Orthodoxy reviled by the Western press!

The present anti-Russian campaign by those who provide the West with its information is beginning to flourish even in the foremost American newspapers and journals and it is of the greatest value and comfort to Soviet communism (although I do not wish to insist that the whole campaign is necessarily Soviet-inspired).

For the West, on the other hand, this campaign stands the facts on their head, inducing it to fear its natural ally—the oppressed Russian people—and to trust its mortal foe, the communist regime. The West is persuaded to send this regime lavish aid, which it so badly needs after half a century of economic bankruptcy.

[11] The "Christian Committee" was formed in 1976. [Tr. note]

[12] Fr. Gleb Yakunin, a founding member of the "Christian Committee" and an outspoken critic of the compliant policies of the Moscow Patriarchate, was arrested in November 1979.

Fr. Dimitri Dudko brought hundreds of persons, including many students and intellectuals, into the Russian Orthodox Church, largely through his remarkable sermons. He was arrested in January 1980. [Tr. note]

[13] In 1974 Aleksandr Ogorodnikov launched a study group in Moscow for the discussion of religious and philosophical issues. The idea caught on in university circles and soon similar Christian seminars were organized in Leningrad, Smolensk, and other cities. Ogorodnikov was arrested in 1978, several other leading figures in 1979. [Tr. note]

6.

When Is Communism in the Saddle?

But even a humbled, defeated, and despoiled nation continues to exist physically, and the aim of the communist authorities (whether in the U.S.S.R., in China, or in Cuba) is to force the people to serve them unfailingly as a work force or, if need be, as a fighting force. However, when it comes to war, communist ideology has long since lost all its drawing power in the U.S.S.R.; it inspires no one. The regime's intention is thus obvious: to take that same Russian national sentiment which they themselves have been persecuting and to exploit it once more for their new war, for their brutal imperialistic ambitions; indeed, to do so with ever greater frenzy and desperation as communism grows ideologically moribund, in a bid to derive from national sentiments the strength and fortitude they lack. This is certainly a real danger.

The informants discussed earlier see this danger, indeed they recognize nothing *but* this danger (rather than the true

37

aspirations of the national spirit). Hence, at their bluntest they abuse us in advance as chauvinists and fascists, while at their most circumspect they argue as follows: Since you can see that any religious and national renascence of the Russian people may be exploited by the Soviet authorities for their own vile purposes, you must renounce not only this renascence but any national aspirations whatever.

But then the Soviet authorities also try to exploit the Jewish emigration from the U.S.S.R. in order to fan the flames of anti-Semitism, and not without success ("See that? They're the only ones allowed to escape from this hell, and the West sends goods to pay for it!"). Does it follow that we are entitled to advise Jews to forgo the quest for their spiritual and national origins? Of course not. Are we not all entitled to live our natural life on the earth and to strive toward our individual goals, without heed for what others may think or what the papers may write, and without worrying about the dark forces that may attempt to exploit those goals for their own ends?

And why should we speak only about the future? We have our recent past to draw on. In 1918–1922 throughout Russia, throngs of peasants with pitchforks (and even in some recorded cases bearing only icons) marched in their thousands against the machine guns of the Red Army; in Bolshevism they saw a force inimical to their very existence as a nation. And in their thousands they were slaughtered.

And what of 1941–1945? It was then that communism first succeeded in saddling and bridling Russian nationalism: millions of lives were affected and it took place in full view of the rest of the world; the murderer saddled his half-dead victim, but in America or Britain no one was appalled; the whole Western world responded with unanimous enthusiasm, and "Russia" was forgiven for all the unpleasant associations her name aroused and for all past sins and omissions. For the first time she became the object of infatuation and applause (paradoxically, even as she ceased being herself), because this saddle horse was then saving the Western world from Hitler. Nor did we hear any reproaches about this being the "supreme danger," although that is in fact precisely what it was. At the time, the West refused even to entertain the thought that the Russians might have any feelings other than communist ones.

But what were the real feelings of the peoples under Soviet dominion? Here is how it was. June 22, 1941, had just reverberated into history, Old Man Stalin had sobbed out his bewildered speech,[14] and the entire working population of adult age and of whatever nationality (not the younger generation, cretinized by Marxism) held its breath in anticipation: Our bloodsuckers have had it! We'll soon be free now. This damned communism is done for! Lithuania, Latvia, and Estonia gave the Germans a jubilant welcome. Byelorussia, the Western Ukraine, and the first occupied Russian territories followed suit. But the mood of the people was demonstrated most graphically of all by the Red Army: before the eyes of the whole world it retreated along a 2,000-kilometer front, on foot, but every bit as fast as motorized units. Nothing could possibly be more convincing than the way

[14] On July 3, 1941, almost two weeks after Germany's attack on the U.S.S.R., Stalin made his first wartime radio address to the nation. In a voice heavy with emotion, he addressed his listeners as "brothers and sisters" and "friends." [Tr. note]

39

these men, soldiers in their prime, voted with their feet. Numerical superiority was entirely with the Red Army, they had excellent artillery and a strong tank force, yet back they rolled, a rout without compare, unprecedented in the annals of Russian and world history. In the first few months some three million officers and men had fallen into enemy hands!

That is what the popular mood was like—the mood of peoples some of whom had lived through twenty-four years of communism and others but a single year.[15] For them the whole point of this latest war was to cast off the scourge of communism. Naturally enough, each people was primarily bent not on resolving any European problem but on its own national task—liberation from communism.

Did the West see this catastrophic retreat? It could not do otherwise. But did it learn any lessons from it? No, blinded by its own pains and anxieties, it has failed to grasp the point to this very day. Yet if it had been unflinchingly committed to the principle of *universal* liberty, it should not have used Lend-Lease to buy the murderous Stalin's help, and should not have strengthened his dominion over nations which were seeking their own freedom. The West should have opened an independent front against Hitler and crushed him by *its own* efforts. The democratic countries had the strength to achieve this, but they grudged it, preferring to shield themselves with the unfortunate peoples of the U.S.S.R.

After twenty-four years of terror, no amount of persuasion could have enabled communism to save its skin by sad-

---

[15] A number of countries and territories were annexed by the U.S.S.R. in 1939–1940. These included Western Ukraine and Western Byelorussia (detached from Poland in 1939), Estonia, Latvia, Lithuania, Northern Bukovina, and Bessarabia. [Tr. note]

dling Russian nationalism. But as it turned out (deprived of outside information in the hermetically sealed communist world, we had no way of anticipating this), another, similar scourge was bearing down on us from the West, one, moreover, with its own special anti-national mission: to annihilate the Russian people in part and to enslave the survivors. And the first thing the Germans did was to restore the collective farms (whose members had scattered in all directions) in order to exploit the peasantry more efficiently. Thus the Russian people were caught between hammer and anvil; faced with two ferocious adversaries, they were bound to favor the one who spoke their own language. Thus was our nationalism forced to don the saddle and bridle of communism. At a stroke, communism seemed to forget its own slogans and doctrines, remaining deaf to them for several years to come; it forgot Marxism, whereas phrases about "glorious Russia" never left its lips; it even went so far as to restore the Church—but all this lasted only until the end of the war. And so our victory in this ill-starred war served only to tighten the yoke about our necks.

But there was also a Russian movement which sought a third path: attempting to take advantage of this war and in spite of the odds to liberate Russia from communism. Such men were in no sense supporters of Hitler; their integration into his empire was involuntary and in their hearts they regarded only the Western countries as their allies (moreover, they felt this sincerely, with none of the duplicity of the communists). For the West, however, anyone who wanted to liberate himself from communism in that war was regarded as a traitor to the cause of the West. Every nation in the

41

U.S.S.R. could be wiped out for all the West cared, and any number of millions could die in Soviet concentration camps, just as long as it could get out of this war successfully and as quickly as possible. And so hundreds of thousands of these Russians and Cossacks, Tatars and Caucasian nationals were sacrificed; they were not even allowed to surrender to the Americans, but were turned over to the Soviet Union, there to face reprisals and execution.

Even more shocking is the way the British and American armies surrendered into the vengeful hands of the communists hundreds of thousands of peaceful civilians, convoys of old men, women, and children, as well as ordinary Soviet POWs and forced laborers used by the Germans—surrendered them against their will, and even after witnessing the suicide of some of them. And British units shot, bayoneted, and clubbed these people who for some reason did not wish to return to their homeland. More amazing still is the fact that not only were none of these British and American officers ever punished or reprimanded, but for almost thirty years the free, proud, and unfettered press of these two countries unanimously and with studied innocence kept its silence about their governments' act of treachery. For thirty years not a single honest pen presented itself! Surely this is the most astonishing fact of all! In this single instance the West's unbroken tradition of publicity suddenly failed. Why?

At the time, it seemed more advantageous to buy off the communists with a couple of million foolish people and in this way to purchase perpetual peace.

In the same way—and without any real need—the whole of Eastern Europe was sacrificed to Stalin.

Now, thirty-five years later, we can sum up the cost of this wisdom: the security of the West today is solely dependent upon the unforeseen Sino-Soviet rift.

7.

A Succession of Errors

The selfish and ruinous mistake that the West committed during World War II has since been repeated time and time again, always in the fervent hope of avoiding a confrontation with communism. The West has done its utmost to ignore communist mass murder and aggression. It promptly forgave East Berlin (1953) as well as Budapest and Prague. It hastened to believe in the peaceful intentions of North Korea (which will yet show its true worth) and in the nobility of North Vietnam. It has allowed itself to be shamefully duped over the Helsinki agreement (for which it paid by recognizing forever all the communist takeovers in Europe). It seized on the myth of a progressive Cuba (even Angola, Ethiopia, and South Yemen have not sufficed to disenchant Senator McGovern), and put its faith in the alleged key to salvation represented by Eurocommunism. It solemnly participated in the interminable sessions of the sham Vienna Conference on European Disarmament. And after April 1978, it tried for almost two years not to notice the seizure of Afghanistan. Historians and future observers will be amazed

45

and at a loss to explain such cowardly blindness. Only the appalling Cambodian genocide has exposed to the West the depth of the lethal abyss (familiar to us, who have lived there for sixty years), but even here, it seems, the Western conscience is already becoming inured and distracted.

It is high time for all starry-eyed dreamers to realize that the nature of communism is one and the same the whole world over, that it is everywhere inimical to the national welfare, invariably striving to destroy the national organism in which it is developing, before moving on to destroy adjacent organisms. No matter what the illusions of détente, no one will ever achieve a stable peace with communism, which is capable only of voracious expansion. Whatever the latest act in the charade of détente, communism continues to wage an incessant ideological war in which the West is unfailingly referred to as the enemy. Communism will never desist from its efforts to seize the world, be it through direct military conquest, through subversion and terrorism, or by subtly undermining society from within. Italy and France are still free, but they have already allowed themselves to be corroded by powerful communist parties. Every human being and any society (especially a democracy) tries to hope for the best; this is only natural. But in the case of communism, there is simply nothing to hope for: no reconciliation with communist doctrine is possible. The alternatives are either its complete triumph throughout the world or else its total collapse everywhere. The only salvation for Russia, for China, and for the entire world lies in a renunciation of this doctrine. Otherwise the world will face inexorable ruin. The communist occupation of Eastern Europe and East Asia will

46

not come to an end; indeed there is an imminent danger of a takeover in Western Europe and many other parts of the world. The prospects for communism in Latin America and Africa have already been clearly demonstrated; in fact, any country that is not careful can be seized. There is of course the hope that things will turn out differently: that the communist aggressors will ultimately fail, like all aggressors in the past. They themselves believe that their hour of world conquest has arrived, and scenting victory, they unwittingly hasten—to their doom. But to achieve such an outcome in a future war would cost mankind billions of casualties.

In view of this mortal danger, one might have thought that American diplomatic efforts would be directed above all toward reducing the threatening might of these imperialistic "horsemen," to ensuring that they will never again succeed in bridling the national feelings of any country and drawing upon the vitality of its people. Yet this path has not been followed; in fact, the opposite course of action has been pursued.

American diplomacy over the last thirty-five years presents a spectacle of sorry bumbling. The United States, only recently the dominant world power, the victor in World War II and the leader in the United Nations, has seen a steady, rapid, and often humiliating erosion of its position at the U.N. and in the world at large, a process even its Western European allies have come to condone. It has continually declined vis-à-vis the U.S.S.R.: things have reached the point where American senators make apologetic visits to Moscow in order to ensure that the debates in the Senate are not taken amiss in the Kremlin. The whole thrust of American diplomacy has been directed to postponing any conflict, even at the cost of progressively diminishing American strength.

The lesson of World War II is that only desperate, pitiless circumstances can bring about any cooperation between communism and the nation it has enslaved. The United States has not learned this lesson: the Soviet and Eastern European governments have been treated as the genuine spokesmen of the national aspirations of the peoples they have subjugated, and the false representatives of these regimes have been dealt with respectfully. This amounts to a rejection—in advance, and in a form most detrimental to American interests—of any future alliance with the oppressed peoples, who are thereby driven firmly into the clutches of communism. This policy leaves the Russian and the Chinese people in bitter and desperate isolation—something the Russians already tasted in 1941.

In the 1950s, an eminent representative of the postwar Russian emigration submitted to the U.S. Administration a project for coordinating the efforts of Russian anti-communist forces. The response was formulated by a high-ranking American official: "We have no need of any kind of Russia, whether future or past." A conceited, mindless, and suicidal answer as far as American interests are concerned. The world has now come to the point where without the rebirth of a healthy, national-minded Russia, America itself will not survive, since all would be annihilated in the bloody clash. In that struggle it would be ruinous for America to fail to distinguish, in theory and in practice, between the communist aggressors and the peoples of the U.S.S.R. so tragically drawn into the conflict. It would be disastrous to fight "the Russians" instead of communism and thereby force a repetition of 1941, when the Russians will again grasp at freedom and find no helping hand.

The day-to-day implementation of current American foreign policy has served to support this perverse and pernicious surrender of the Russian national consciousness to its communist taskmaster. And now, after thirty-five years of failure, American diplomacy has gambled on another short-sighted, unwise—indeed mad—policy: to use China as a shield, which means in effect abandoning the national forces of China as well, and driving them completely under the communist yoke. (In the interests of this policy it was even deemed acceptable to contribute Taiwan as a down payment.)

This act of betrayal is a blow to the national feelings of both Chinese *and* Russians. ("America is openly supporting our totalitarian oppressors and equipping them against us!")

I hardly dare ask where that leaves the principles of democracy. Where is the vaunted respect for the freedom of all nations? But even in purely strategic terms this is a short-sighted policy: a fateful reconciliation of the two communist regimes could occur overnight, at which point they could unite in turning against the West. But even without such a reconciliation, a China armed by America would be more than a match for America.

The strategic error of not realizing that the oppressed peoples are allies of the West has led Western governments to commit a number of irreparable blunders. For many years they could have had free access to the oppressed people via the airwaves. But this means was either not used at all or else used incompetently. It would have been an easy matter for America to relay television broadcasts to the Soviet Union via satellite, but it was easier still to abandon this project after angry protests from the Soviet regime (which knows what to fear). It goes without saying that this medium would require a proper appreciation for the needs and intellectual concerns of the suffering people to whom it is addressed. And it also goes without saying that offensive commercial broadcasts are not what is needed—this would merely be an affront to the hungry viewers, and would be worse than nothing.

The defective information about the U.S.S.R. that reaches America brings about a mutual lack of communication, and as a result Americans, too, find it difficult to understand what they look like from the other side. A case in point is the Russian section of the Voice of America, which seems to go out of its way to repel the thoughtful Russian listener from any understanding of America, to alienate his sympathies, and even to shock and distress him.

The West is incapable of creating balanced and effective broadcasts to the Soviet Union precisely because information about the U.S.S.R. is received in the West in skewed and distorted form. The Russian section of the Voice of America, with its large staff and considerable budget, serves American interests poorly, in fact frequently does them great disservice. Apart from news and topical political commentary, hours of the daily program are filled with trite and inconsequential drivel which can do nothing but irritate the hungry and oppressed millions of listeners whose paramount need is to be told the truth about their own history. Instead of transmitting this history to them (with frequent repetition to compensate for the difficulties of radio reception), together with readings from those books the very possession of which is punishable by imprisonment in the U.S.S.R., instead of bolstering the anti-communist spirit of these potential allies of the U.S.A., hours of radio time are filled with frivolous reports on enthusiastic collectors of beer bottles and on the delights of ocean cruises (the fine food, the casino and discotheque are described with particular relish), with biographical details about American pop singers, any amount of sports news, which the citizens of the U.S.S.R. are not prevented from knowing anyway, and jazz, which they can pick up without difficulty from any of the other foreign stations. (Hardly more felicitous is the policy of broadcasting accounts by recent Jewish immigrants to the U.S.A., who tell in great detail about their life, their new jobs, and about how happy they are here. Since it is common knowledge in the U.S.S.R. that only Jews have the right to emigrate, these programs serve no purpose except to further the growth of anti-Semitism.) It is clear that the directors of the Voice of America are constantly trying not to arouse the anger of the Soviet leadership. In their zeal to serve détente, they remove from their programs everything that might irritate the communists in power. There are plenty of examples of such political kowtowing to the Central Committee of the CPSU, but I will cite two instances from my own experience, simply because they are easier for me to document. My statement concerning the arrest of Alexander Ginzburg on 4 February 1977 consisted of only three sentences, of which the following two were cut by the censors at VOA:

> This reprisal affects people in the West far more than it might seem at first sight. It is a significant step in the unremitting and all-inclusive policy of securing the Soviet rear in order to facilitate the offensive operation which it has been conducting so successfully over the last few years and which can only be intensified in the future: an assault on the strength, spirit, and the very existence of the West.

My statement to the 1977 Sakharov Hearings in Rome was completely rejected by VOA because of the following passage:

> ... [I would like] to hope that the spine-chilling accounts heard from your rostrum might pierce the deafness of material well-being which will respond only to the trumpet of doom but heeds no lesser sound. May they penetrate the awareness of those short-sighted individuals who are content to relax and to bask in the venomous melodies of Eurocommunism.

The chaste guardians of the VOA could not permit such words to reach the ears of its listeners in the East, or, for that matter, in the West. But this is not the worst of it: at times the Voice of America dances to the tune called by the communist regime or indeed becomes indistinguishable from a Moscow radio station. A recent broadcast apropos of Tito's illness announced that there was also "joyful news" to report from Yugoslavia: in the days of their leader's illness, thousands of citizens are eagerly joining the Party! Is this really any different from the insulting Leninist-Stalinist drivel that blares forth every day from Soviet loudspeakers? Such a broadcast can only cause Soviet listeners to doubt the mental competence of those who transmit it. And the religious program almost completely excludes Orthodox services, which are what Russian listeners most need, deprived as they are of churches. In the meager time slot available to religion as a whole, Orthodoxy is curtailed (as it is curtailed in the U.S.S.R.) because it is "a religion uncharacteristic of the U.S.A." This may be so, but it is surely characteristic of Russia! And the broadcast *is* conducted in Russian.

If we add to this the fact that the broadcasts are presented in a language difficult to acknowledge as Russian (replete with crude grammatical errors, poor syntax, inadequate enunciation, and misplaced stress), then it is fair to conclude that every reasonable effort has been made to turn away Russian listeners from this radio station.

This is an inept utilization of the mightiest weapon that the United States possesses to create mutual understanding (or even an alliance) between America and the oppressed Russian people.

It is true that other Western Russian-language radio stations have similar defects. The BBC, too, shows a marked eagerness not to offend communist sensibilities and a superficial understanding of the Russian people of today; this leads to an inability to select what is genuinely important for its listeners, and many valuable hours of broadcasting time are taken up with worthless and irrelevant twaddle.

8.

What My *Letter to the Soviet Leaders* Attempted to Do

For the multinational human mass confined today within the boundaries of the Soviet Union, there are only two possibilities: either a brutally imperialistic development of communism, with the subjugation of countries in many parts of the globe, or else a renunciation of communist ideology and a shift to a path of reconciliation, recovery, love of one's country, and care for one's people.

As a Russian, I find little consolation in the thought that Soviet communism might after all suffer defeat in the pursuit of the first alternative, and that a certain number of today's bosses (those who fail to make a getaway) will face a military tribunal on the Nuremberg model. There is no comfort in this thought because the human cost of achieving this outcome would fall most heavily on the deceived and afflicted Russian people.

But how to make the second alternative attainable? It is extraordinarily difficult to achieve such an outcome with in-

[handwritten annotation in margin: "people never leave the top"? and "could we continue to be if good, well-intentioned"]

digenous strength alone in the conditions of a communist dictatorship, especially because the rest of the world, in its blindness, shows little sympathy for our attempts to free ourselves from communism, and at best washes its hands of us.

When I came to understand this problem, I decided seven years ago to undertake an action which it was within my limited powers to accomplish: I wrote my *Letter to the Soviet Leaders*, in which I call on them to shake off the communist delirium and to minister to their own devastated country.[16] The chances of success were naturally almost nil, but my aim was at least to pose the question loudly and publicly. If not the current leaders, then perhaps one of their successors might take note of my proposals. In the *Letter* I attempted to formulate the minimum national policy that could be implemented without wresting power from the incumbent communist rulers. (It would surely have been entirely unrealistic to expect them to relinquish their personal power.) I proposed that they should discard communist ideology, at least for the time being. (But how painful it would be to renounce this weapon, insomuch as it is precisely to communist ideas that the West yields most readily! . . .)

In the sphere of foreign policy, my proposal foresaw the following consequences: We were not to "concern ourselves with the fortunes of other hemispheres," we were to "renounce unattainable and irrelevant missions of world domination," to "give up our Mediterranean aspirations," and to "abandon the financing of South American revolutionaries." Africa should be left in peace; Soviet troops should be with-

[16] The *Letter* was sent to its addressees in September 1973. The Russian text and its English translation were published in 1974. [Tr. note]

56

drawn from Eastern Europe (so that these puppet regimes would be left to face their own people without the support of Soviet divisions); no peripheral nation should be forcibly kept within the bounds of our country; the youth of Russia should be liberated from universal, compulsory military service. As I wrote: "The demands of internal growth are incomparably more important to us, as a people, than the need for any external expansion of our power."

The reaction of the addressees to my proposal was hardly surprising: they didn't bat an eye. But the reaction of the Western and in particular the American press simply astonished me. My program was construed as conservative, retrograde, isolationist, and as a tremendous threat to the world! It would seem that the consciousness of the West has been so debilitated by decades of capitulation that when the Soviet Union, after seizing half of Europe, ventures into Asia and Africa, this evokes respect: we must not anger them, we must try to find a common language with these progressive forces (no doubt a confusion with "aggressive" here). Yet when I called for an immediate halt to all aggression, and to any thought of aggression, when I proposed that all those peoples who so wished should be free to secede, and that the Soviet Union should look to its domestic problems, this was interpreted as and even noisily proclaimed to be reactionary and dangerous isolationism. *ridiculous !*

But at the very least, one should be able to draw a distinction between the isolationism of the world's chief defender (the United States) and the isolationism of the world's major assailant (the Soviet Union). The former withdrawal is certainly a grave danger to the world and to peace in general, while the latter would be highly beneficial. If Soviet (and to-day also Cuban and Vietnamese, tomorrow Chinese) troops would cease taking over the world and would go home, whom would this endanger? Could someone explain this to me? I cannot understand to this day.

Furthermore, I never proposed any kind of total isolation-ism (involving cultural and economic withdrawal, for in-stance), nor did I call for Russia to sequester herself as if there were no one else on the globe. To my nation—an or-ganism gravely ill after sixty years of communism and after sixty million human victims (not counting war casualties)—I offered the only advice that can be offered to someone so se-riously afflicted: Stop wasting your valuable strength on fighting and pushing around healthy people; concentrate on your own recovery, conserving to this end every grain of the nation's strength. "Let us find strength, sense and courage to put our own house in order before we busy ourselves with the cares of the entire planet"; "the physical and spiritual health of the people must be the goal." I envisaged an ascent from the material and moral abyss in which the people find themselves today. Children were to be preserved from hav-ing their heads stuffed with ideology, women were to be shielded from backbreaking physical labor, men saved from alcohol, and nature protected from poison; the shattered family upbringing was to be restored; schools were to be im-proved and the Russian language itself saved before it could be destroyed by the communist system. To achieve all this would require some 150 to 200 years of external peace and patient concentration on internal problems. Whom could this possibly endanger?

But this letter was a genuine address to very real rulers

possessed of immeasurable power, and it was plain that the very most one could hope for would be concessions on their side, certainly not capitulation: neither free general elections nor a complete (or even partial) change of leadership could be expected. The most I called for was a renunciation of communist ideology and of its most cruel consequences, so as to allow at least a little more breathing space for the national spirit, for throughout history only national-minded individuals have been able to make constructive contributions to society. And the only path down from the icy cliff of totalitariansim that I could propose was the slow and smooth descent via an authoritarian system. (If an unprepared people were to jump off that cliff directly into democracy, it would be crushed to an anarchical pulp.) This "authoritarianism" of mine also drew immediate fire in the Western press.

But in the *Letter* I qualified this concept then and there: "an authoritarian order founded on love of one's fellow man"; "an authoritarianism with a firm basis in laws that reflect the will of the people"; "a calm and stable system" which does not "degenerate into arbitrariness and tyranny"; a renunciation, "once and for all, of psychiatric violence and secret trials, and of that brutal, immoral trap which the camps represent"; the toleration of all religions; "free art and literature, the untrammeled publication of books." I doubt that anyone can offer any temporary measures more beneficial than these to take effect after we emerge from our prison.

As concerns the theoretical question whether Russia should choose or reject authoritarianism in the future, I have no final opinion, and have not offered any. My criticism of certain aspects of democracy is well known. I do not think that the will of the English people was implemented when England was for years sapped of its strength by a Labor government—elected by only forty percent of the voters. Nor was the will of the German people served when the Left bloc had a majority of one seat in the Bundestag. Nor is any nation served when half the electorate is so disillusioned that it stays away from the polling booths. I cannot count among the virtues of democracy its impotence vis-à-vis small groups of terrorists, its inability to prevent the growth of organized crime, or to check unrestrained profiteering at the expense of public morality. And I would note that the terrifying phenomenon of totalitarianism, which has been born into our world perhaps four times, did not issue from authoritarian systems, but in each case from a weak democracy: the one created by the February Revolution in Russia, the Weimar and the Italian republics, and Chiang Kai-shek's China. The majority of governments in human history have been authoritarian, but they have yet to give birth to a totalitarian regime.

I have never attempted to analyze this whole question in theoretical terms, nor do I intend to do so now, for I am neither a political scientist nor a politician. I am simply an artist who is distressed by the painfully clear events and crises of today. And in any case the problem cannot, I think, be settled by any journalistic debate or any hasty advice, even if it be buttressed by scholarship. The answer can only emerge through an organic development of accumulated national experience, and it must be free of any external coercion.

Here I would like to point once more to the respectful consideration which scholarship has always accorded the various unique features in the cultural development of even the smallest nations of Africa or Asia. And I would simply ask that the Russian people not be denied the same kind of treatment and that we not be dictated to, just as Africa is not. The Russian people have a 1,100-year-long history— longer than that of many of Russia's impatient teachers. Over this long period the Russians have created a large store of their own traditional social concepts, which outside observers should not dismiss with a sneer. Here are a few examples. The traditional medieval Russian concept of justice (*pravda*)[17] was understood as justice in the ultimate sense. It was an ontological rather than a juridical concept, something granted by God. The social ideal was to live justly (*pravedno*), that is, live on a higher moral plane than any possible legal requirement. (This of course does not mean that everyone lived up to such precepts, but the ideal was accepted by all.) A number of Russian proverbs reflect this concern:

> The world itself weighs less than one just word (*odno slovo pravdy*).
> The Lord resides in justice (*v pravde*), not in strength.
> If all men lived justly (*po pravde*), no laws would be needed.

According to another traditional Russian concept, the truth cannot be determined by voting, since the majority does not necessarily have any deeper insight into the truth. (And

[17] In modern Russian, this word means "truth." In medieval Russia, this term signified "justice," "right," as well as "law" in the broad sense. The first Russian code of laws (eleventh century) was called *Pravda Russkaya*. [Tr. note]

what we know of mass psychology would suggest that the reverse is often true.) When representatives of the entire country gathered for important decisions (the so-called Assemblies of the Land), there was no voting. Truth was sought by a lengthy process of mutual persuasion, and it was determined when final accord was reached. While the decision of the Assembly was not legally binding on the tsar, it was morally incontestable. From this perspective, the creation of *parties*, that is, of segments or parts which fight for their *partial interests* at the expense of the other segments of the people, seems an absurdity. (Indeed this is less than worthy of mankind, at least of mankind in its potential.)

It is no accident that the powerful regime before which the free world trembles (including the free Western leaders, legislators, and journalists) has made no effort more concentrated and ferocious in sixty years than its attempt to eradicate Christianity—the world view of its subjugated country. And yet they have proved incapable of destroying it!

And at this time the latest informants hasten to persuade the West that this ever-vital Christianity is in fact the greatest danger.

9.

Some Words of Explanation

Any public statement with social or political overtones always elicits a great deal of comment, much of it sober and scrupulous, but the distorted reactions are invariably the loudest, they acquire hysterical headlines and attempt to imprint themselves on the memory, not without occasional success. My way of life, my work habits, and principles of behavior usually preclude any response on my part to all this cacophony. But now that I have touched upon some issues of consequence, I would like very briefly to comment on a number of distortions.

Apropos of my *Letter to the Soviet Leaders* and on other occasions since then, I have been repeatedly charged with being an advocate of a theocratic state, a system in which the government would be under the direct control of religious leaders. This is a flagrant misrepresentation; I have never said or written anything of the sort. The day-to-day activity of governing in no sense belongs to the sphere of religion. What I do believe is that the state should not persecute religion, and that, furthermore, religion should make an appropriate contribution to the spiritual life of the nation. Such a situation obtains in Poland and Israel and no one condemns it; I cannot understand why the same thing should be forbidden to Russia—a land that has carried its faith through ten centuries and earned the right to it by sixty years of suffering and the blood of millions of laymen and tens of thousands of clergy.

At the same time I was accused of propounding some kind of "way back"; one must think a man a fool to ascribe to him the desire to move against the flow of time. It was alleged that I am asking the future Russia "to renounce modern technology." Another fabrication: I had in fact called for "highly developed technology," albeit "on a small, non-gigantic scale."

The path that I do propose is set forth in the conclusion of my Harvard speech and I can repeat it here: there is no other way left but—*upward.* I believe that the lavishly materialistic twentieth century has all too long kept us in a subhuman state—some of us through superabundance, others through hunger.

The Harvard speech rewarded me with an outpouring of favorable responses from the American public at large (some of these found their way into newspapers). For that reason I was not perturbed by the outburst of reproaches that an angry press rained down upon me. I had not expected it to be so unreceptive to criticism: I was called a fanatic, a man possessed, a mind split apart, a cynic, a vindictive warmonger; I was even simply told to "get out of the country" (a fine way of applying the principle of free speech, but hardly distinguishable from Soviet practice). There were indignant questions about how I dare use the phrase "our country" in reference to the one that banished me. (The point of course is that the communist government, not Russia, had deported me.) Richard Pipes brought up the "freedom of speech which so annoys Solzhenitsyn." In fact, it was stated plainly enough for all who can read that I had in mind not freedom of speech, but only the irresponsible and amoral abuse of this freedom.

But the most widespread allegation was that I "call upon the West" to liberate our people from the communists. This could not have been said by anyone who had made a conscientious effort to read and comprehend the text. I have never made any such appeal either in my Harvard address or at any time before that, indeed never once in all my public statements over the years have I appealed for help to a single Western government or parliament. I have always maintained that we shall liberate *ourselves*, that it is *our own* task, difficult as it may be. To the West I have made but one request and offered but one word of advice. First the request: please do not force us into the grip of dictatorship, do not betray millions of our countrymen as you did in 1945, and do not use your technological resources to further strengthen our oppressors. And the advice: take care lest your headlong retreat lead you into a pit from which there is no climbing out.

After the Harvard speech, some members of the press asked with feigned surprise how I could defend the "right not to know." As a rule, they cut the quotation short, omitting: "not to have their divine souls stuffed with gossip, nonsense, vain talk." My answer is already expressed in that omitted passage. They pointed out reproachfully that this is the same Solzhenitsyn who when in the U.S.S.R. struggled for the right *to know.* Yes, I did struggle for the right of the whole world to know—about the Gulag Archipelago, about the popular resistance to communism, about the millions of dead, about the famine of 1933 and the treachery of 1945. But we who have lived through these grim years are pained when the press offers us gratuitous details about a former British Prime Minister who has undergone surgery on one testicle, about the kind of blanket Jacqueline Kennedy uses, or about the favorite drink of some female pop star.

A more serious misunderstanding arose from the passage where I said that the deadly crush of life in the East has developed greater depth of character than the well-ordered life of the West. Some bewildered commentators interpreted this as praise for the virtues of communism and an assertion of the spiritual superiority of the Soviet system. Of course I meant no such thing. This is no more than the ancient truth that strength of character comes from suffering and adversity. Oppressed and driven as they are by constant poverty, it is inevitable that many of our people are crushed, debased, warped, or dehumanized. But evil that bears down openly upon men corrupts less insidiously than does the furtive, seductive variety of evil. Direct oppression can give birth to a contrary process too—a process of spiritual ascent, even of soaring flight. Russian faces seldom if ever wear a token smile, but we are more generous in our support of one another. This is all done voluntarily and informally, and such sacrifices are in no sense tax deductible; indeed no such system even exists in our country. Taking risks for the sake of others is part of the moral climate in which we live, and I have more than once had occasion to witness the transformation which people from the West have undergone after living and working for a long period in Soviet conditions. It was reported that one American reader had offered his daughters one hundred dollars each to read the second volume of *The Gulag Archipelago*—but that the girls had refused. In our country, on the other hand, people read it even under threat of imprisonment. Or compare two young people—one a cowardly terrorist in Western Europe turning his bombs against peaceful citizens and a democratic government, the other a dissident in Eastern Europe stepping forth with bare hands against the dragon of communism. Compare, too, young Americans anxious to avoid the draft with the young Soviet soldiers who refused to fire upon insurgents—in Berlin, in Budapest, or in Afghanistan—and who were summarily executed (as they knew they would be!).

I can envision no salvation for mankind other than through the universal exercise of self-limitation by individuals and peoples alike. That is the spirit which imbues the religious and national renascence currently under way in Russia. It is something that I put forward as my fundamental belief in an essay entitled "Repentance and Self-Limitation in the Life of Nations," published five years ago in America.[18] For some reason, my opponents avoid mentioning this essay or quoting from it.

Not long ago *The New York Review of Books* carried a prominent and ominous headline: "The Dangers of Solzhenitsyn's Nationalism." But neither the journal nor its infor-

[18] In *From Under the Rubble* (Boston-Toronto: Little, Brown, 1975).

mants had the wit to indicate in the essay thus advertised where exactly these dangers lay. Well, then, I shall help them out with some quotations from my published writings.

From my *Letter to the Soviet Leaders:*[19]

"I wish all people well, and the closer they are to us and the more dependent upon us, the more fervent is my wish." (p. 7)

"One aches with sympathy for the ordinary Chinese too, because it is they who will be the most helpless victims of the war." (p. 16)

From my essay on "Repentance and Self-Limitation" in *From Under the Rubble:*

"We shall have to find in ourselves the resolve . . . to acknowledge our *external* sins, those against other peoples." (p. 128)

"With regard to all the peoples in and beyond our borders forcibly drawn into our orbit, we can fully purge our guilt [only] by giving them genuine freedom to decide their future for themselves." (p. 135)

"Just as it is impossible to build a good society when relations between people are bad, there will never be a good world while nations are on bad terms and secretly cherish the desire for revenge. . . . Among states too the moral rule for individuals will be adopted—do not unto others as you would not have done unto you." (pp. 134, 137)

So there you have the danger of "Solzhenitsyn's nationalism." This is the threat of the Russian religious and national revival.

[19] Aleksandr Solzhenitsyn, *Letter to the Soviet Leaders* (New York: Harper & Row, 1974).

10.

One Step from the Brink

Today Afghanistan, yesterday Czechoslovakia and Angola, tomorrow some other Soviet takeover—yet even after all this, how good it would be to go on believing in détente! Could it really be over? "But the Soviet leaders haven't repudiated it at all! Brezhnev was quite clear about that: it was in *Pravda!*" (Thus Marshall Shulman and other, like-minded experts.)

Yes indeed, the Soviet leaders are quite prepared to carry on détente; why shouldn't they be? This is the same détente that the West basked in so contentedly while millions were being exterminated in the jungles of Cambodia. The same détente that so gladdened Western hearts at a time when a thousand men, including twelve-year-old boys, were being executed in one Afghan village. (And this was surely not a unique case!) We Russians immediately recognize an episode like this. That's the Soviet way of doing things! That's the way they slaughtered us, too, from 1918 on! Détente will continue to stand Soviet communism in very good stead: for the purpose of stifling the last flicker of dissidence in the So-

viet Union and buying up whatever electronic equipment is
necessary.

The West simply does not want to believe that the time
for sacrifices has arrived; it is simply unprepared for sacrifices. Men who go on trading right until the first salvo is
fired are incapable of sacrificing so much as their commercial profits: they have not the wit to realize that their children will never enjoy these gains, that today's illusory profits
will return as tomorrow's devastation. The Western allies are
maneuvering to see who can sacrifice the least. Behind all
this lies that sleek god of affluence, now proclaimed as the
goal of life, replacing the high-minded view of the world
which the West has lost.

Communism will never be halted by negotiations or
through the machinations of détente. It can be halted only
by force from without or by disintegration from within. The
smooth and effortless course of the West's long retreat could
not go on forever, and it is now coming to an end; the brink
may not have been reached, but it is already the merest step
away. Since the outlying borders were never defended, the
nearer ones will have to be held. Today the Western world
faces a greater danger than that which threatened it in 1939.

It would be disastrous for the world if America were to
look upon the Peking leadership as an ally while regarding
the Russian people as no less a foe than communism: by so
doing she would drive both these great nations into the maw
of communism and plunge in after them. She would deprive
both great peoples of their last hope of liberation. The inde-
fatigable denigrators of Russia and all things Russian are for-
getting to check their watches: All of America's mistakes

and misconceptions about Russia might have been purely academic in the past, but not in the swift-moving world of today. On the eve of the global battle between world communism and world humanity, would that the West at least distinguished the enemies of humanity from its friends, and that it sought an alliance not of foes but of friends. So much has been ceded, surrendered, and traded away that today even a fully united Western world can no longer prevail except by allying itself with the captive peoples of the communist world.

Vermont
February 1980